NICK BUTTERWORTH AND MICK INKPEN

STORIES JESUS TOLD

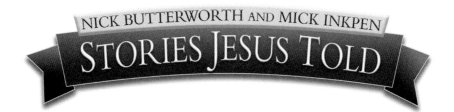

NICK BUTTERWORTH AND MICK INKPEN
STORIES JESUS TOLD

CANDLE
BOOKS

Stories Jesus Told
Text and illustrations copyright © 1994 Nick Butterworth and Mick Inkpen
This edition copyright © 2005 Lion Hudson

Published by Candle Books
an imprint of
Lion Hudson plc
Wilkinson House, Jordan Hill Road,
Oxford OX2 8DR, England
www.lionhudson.com/candle

ISBN 978 1 85985 588 1

First edition 2005

USA edition published by

Zonder**kidz**.

Zonderkidz is a trademark of Zondervan

First published by Marshall, Morgan & Scott in 8 separate volumes under the titles:
The House on the Rock; *The Lost Sheep*; *The Precious Pearl*; *The Two Sons*;
The Ten Silver Coins; *The Rich Farmer*; *The Little Gate* and *The Good Stranger*
by Nick Butterworth and Mick Inkpen.

Acknowledgments
Scripture quotations in this book are taken from the Good News Bible © 1966, 1971,
1976, 1992 American Bible Society.

A catalogue record for this book is available from the British Library.

Printed and bound in Serbia, November 2018, LH55.

Contents

Jesus said, 'Suppose one of you has a hundred sheep and loses one of them – what do you do? You leave the other ninety-nine sheep in the pasture and go looking for the one that got lost until you find it. When you find it, you are so happy that you put it on your shoulders and carry it back home. Then you call your friends and neighbours together and say to them, "I am so happy I found my lost sheep. Let us celebrate!"

In the same way, I tell you, there will be more joy in heaven over one sinner who repents than over ninety-nine respectable people who do not need to repent.'

Luke 15:4–7

The
Lost Sheep

Here is a farmer.

He has a hundred sheep.

He is counting them.

One of his sheep is missing.

Oh dear!

Where has it gone?

Is it in the hen-house?

No.

Is it behind the haystack?

No.

Is it under the hedge?

No, it is lost.

All day the farmer looks for his sheep.

He climbs up hills and scrambles over rocks.

He crawls through bramble
bushes.

The thorns scratch him.

But he will not give up.

He is tired and hungry.

His feet ache.

But he will not give up.

At last, the farmer sees
his sheep.

It has fallen in the river.

The farmer dives into the water.

Splosh!

He rescues the sheep.

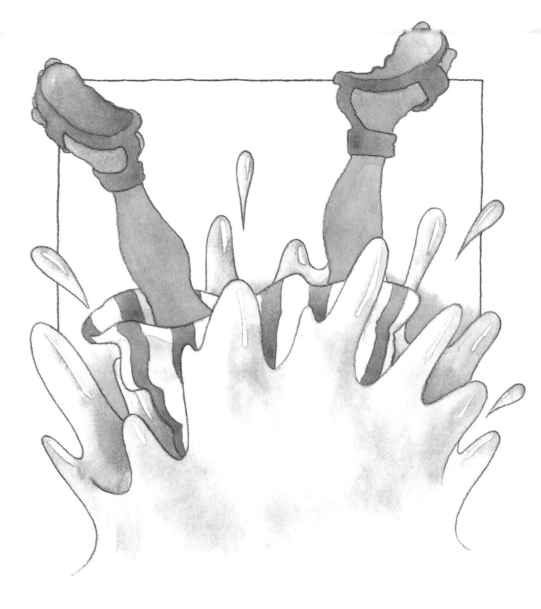

Hooray! The farmer has found his sheep.

Let's all have a party!

Jesus says, 'God is like the farmer. He loves us just like the farmer loves his sheep.'

Jesus said, 'Also, the kingdom of heaven is like this.
A man is looking for fine pearls, and when he finds one that is
unusually fine, he goes and sells everything he has,
and buys that pearl.'

Matthew 13:45–46

The
Precious Pearl

Here is a man who buys and sells things.

He is called a merchant.

He has a fine fur coat and a felt hat with a floppy feather. It is his favourite.

The house he lives in is huge.

It has five floors and a fishpond with a fountain in the front garden.

The merchant has everything he wants.

He has fifteen rooms filled with furniture.

He has four freezers
full of food.

(And three fridges
for fizzy drinks.)

And there is more money under
his mattress than you could
ever imagine. Much more.
Yes, the merchant has everything
he wants, until…

One day, in a shop window, he sees something. Something special.

It is a wonderful white pearl.

'Five hundred thousand pounds,' says the man in the shop.

It is even more money than the merchant has under his mattress. But he wants that pearl more than anything in the world.

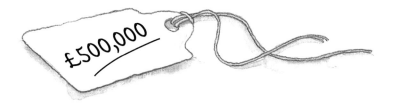

He hurries home. He has a plan. He sells his furniture, his fridges and his freezers full of food.

He sells his house, his fountain and his fishpond.

He sells his fine fur coat.
But the felt hat with the
floppy feather, he keeps.
It is his favourite.

He borrows a barrow and bundles in the money.

Off to the shop he trundles to buy the pearl.

Oh dear! He is still six pounds short.

'Sell me your hat for six pounds,' says the man in the shop.

The merchant laughs.
He hands the man his hat and takes the pearl.

Hooray! The pearl is his at last.

Jesus says, 'God is like the merchant's pearl. It costs everything to know him. But he is worth more than anything in the world.'

Jesus said, 'Now what do you think?
There was once a man who had two sons. He went to the elder
one and said, "Son, go and work in the vineyard today." "I don't
want to," he answered, but later he changed his mind and went.
Then the father went to the other son and said the same thing.
"Yes, sir," he answered, but he did not go. Which one of the two
sons did what his father wanted?'

Matthew 21:28–31

The
Two Sons

Here is a man.

He grows apples in an orchard.

The apples are red and rosy.
It is time for them to be picked.

At home the man has two sons.

'I want you to help me to pick the apples,' says the man to his first son.

'No,' says the first son. 'I'm busy.'

But after a while he is sorry
for what he said.

He picks up a basket and goes
to the orchard.

The man finds his second son.

'I want you to help me pick
the apples too,' he says.

'Yes,' says the second son.
'I will come as soon as I have
put on my boots.'

Back in the orchard the first son is busy picking apples.

Look, he has already filled one basket.

'Well done, son,' says the man.
'Here is another basket.
We'll have this done in no time.'

They work together until all
the apples have been picked.
But there is no sign of the
second son.

He has forgotten his promise.

Who do you think pleased his father?

The first son or the second son?

Jesus says,
'What we do is
more important
than what
we say.'

Jesus said, 'So then, anyone who hears these words of mine and obeys them is like a wise man who built his house on rock. The rain poured down, the rivers overflowed, and the wind blew hard against that house. But it did not fall, because it was built on rock.

'But anyone who hears these words of mine and does not obey them is like a foolish man who built his house on sand. The rain poured down, the rivers overflowed, the wind blew hard against that house, and it fell. And what a terrible fall that was!'

Matthew 7:24–27 and Luke 6:47–49

The House
on the Rock

Here is a man.

He is looking for a place to build a house.

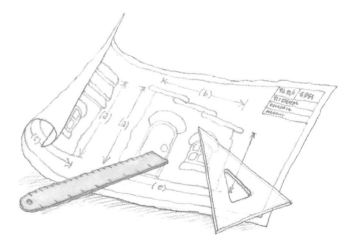

He climbs to the top of a big grey rock.

Ah! Here is a good place.

The man begins to build
his house.

It is hard work.

He puffs and pants.

He puffs and pants and grunts and groans all day, until the work is done.

'Just in time,' he says. 'It looks like rain.'

The rain pours down.

The lightning flashes.

The thunder booms.

The water washes round the house and splashes at the rock.

The rock stays firm.

The man was wise to choose the rock.

Here is another man. He wants a house.

'I want it now. I want it quick. This place will do,' he says.

He builds his house down on the sand.

'This won't take long,' he says, and whistles as he works.

His house is done.

He goes inside and shuts the door.

A raindrop drips onto his nose.
Oh dear!

The rain pours down.

The lightning flashes.

The thunder booms.

The water rushes through the house and splashes at his knees!

The sand is washed away.

His house falls flat.

The silly man was wrong to build on sand.

Jesus says, 'I am like the
wise man's rock. If you trust me,
I will never let you down.'

Jesus said, 'Or suppose a woman who has ten silver coins loses one of them – what does she do?
She lights a lamp, sweeps her house, and looks carefully everywhere until she finds it. When she finds it, she calls her friends and neighbours together, and says to them,
"I am so happy I found the coin I lost. Let us celebrate!"
In the same way, I tell you, the angels of God rejoice over one sinner who repents.'

Luke 15:8–10

The Ten
Silver Coins

Here is a woman. She has
ten silver coins. She likes to
count them.

One, two, three, four...

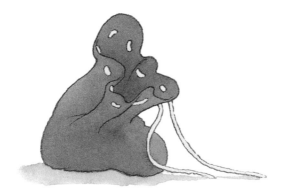

Oops! Silly cat! Now they've gone all over the place.

The woman picks up her silver coins. They have been scattered everywhere!

The cat doesn't care. He has stretched out and gone to sleep.

The woman counts her silver coins again. But there are only nine. Bother! One of them is missing.

Never mind, it can't have gone far.

Perhaps it is under the rug.
No. There is no sign of it there.

Perhaps it has bounced into the fireplace. Carefully she sifts through the ashes.

What a messy job! But no, there is no coin.

Perhaps it rolled right under the door and out into the garden.

She searches and searches, but she cannot find the coin anywhere.

She even looks inside her pots and pans, even though she really knows it can't be there.

Clatter! Bang! What a noise she is making!

She's making so much noise,
she's woken up the cat. Serves
him right. He's off to find a
quiet spot in the garden.

There it is! The cat was lying on it all the time! The missing silver coin is found!

The woman laughs. She is so
happy she calls a friend to
tell her the good news.

Jesus says, 'We are like the woman's silver coins. God wants every single one of us.'

Jesus said, 'It is much harder for a rich person to enter the kingdom of God than for a camel to go through the eye of a needle.'

Mark 10:25

The
Little Gate

Here is a wall which surrounds a town.

In the wall is a little gate. It has a funny name. It is called the Eye of a Needle because it is so small.

One day a camel arrives at the gate.

This is no ordinary camel. He has a fine saddle with red tassles, and his own servant boy to flick away the flies.

He is loaded high with carpets to sell in the market.

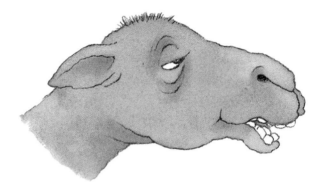

'Make way,' he says, 'I'm coming through!'

But he isn't coming through at all! He can't get through the hole. He is too big!

'Try wriggling through backwards,' says the boy. And he shows the camel how.

'Camels never wriggle,' says
the camel. But just the same,
he turns around and pushes his
bottom into the hole.

He heaves and pushes.
(He even wriggles.)

But it is no good. He cannot
get through the gate.

'I'll unload you,' says the boy. He unties the ropes and takes off all the carpets.

'Now try again.'

It is no use. The camel still cannot squeeze through the gate.

'Your saddle keeps getting stuck,' says the boy. 'You will have to let me take it off.'

Without his fine saddle, the
camel does not look proud and
important any more.

He is just an ordinary camel.

Once more the camel tries.
Down on his knees, shuffling
forward, inch by inch, until
finally…

Hooray! He is through!

Jesus says, 'It is very hard for a rich man to get into heaven. It's easier for a camel to get through the eye of a needle!'

Jesus said, 'There was once a man who was going down from Jerusalem to Jericho when robbers attacked him, stripped him, and beat him up, leaving him half dead. It so happened that a priest was going down that road; but when he saw the man, he walked on by, on the other side. In the same way a Levite also came along, went over and looked at the man, and then walked on by, on the other side.

But a Samaritan who was travelling that way came upon the man, and when he saw him, his heart was filled with pity. He went over to him, poured oil and wine on his wounds and bandaged them; then he put the man on his own animal and took him to an inn, where he took care of him. The next day he took out two silver coins and gave them to the innkeeper. "Take care of him," he told the innkeeper, "and when I come back this way, I will pay you whatever else you spend on him."'

And Jesus concluded, 'In your opinion, which one of these three acted like a neighbour towards the man attacked by the robbers?' The teacher of the Law answered, 'The one who was kind to him.' Jesus replied, 'You go, then, and do the same.'

Luke 10:30–37

The
Good Stranger

Here is a man. He is going on a long journey.

He packs some sandwiches and a flask of tea. Then he climbs onto his donkey.

'Giddyup!'

Soon he has left the town behind him.

The sun is hot and the long climb up into the hills makes his donkey puff.

The path winds between high rocks. It is a dark place, full of shadows.

'I don't like it here,' says the man. He has a funny feeling that someone is watching him.

Suddenly there is a shout!
Robbers! Three of them!

They steal his donkey and
all his belongings. And they
whack him on the head
with his own stick!

Poor man. He is left lying on the path. His head is bleeding and he cannot move his legs.

He lies here for a long time, then, finally he falls asleep.

After a while, someone comes along the path. He is wearing fine clothes. A bishop.

He stops, then hurries past, pretending not to see. Perhaps he is late for important business.

Perhaps he is afraid.

The man wakes up and starts
to call for help.

Ah! Here comes someone.
A man in a wig. A judge.

'Help! Help!'

But the judge pretends not
to hear and he hurries past.
Just like the bishop.

The sun rises high in the sky. The man is hot. His throat is dry. But here come more footsteps! Who is it?

On no! It is a stranger from a foreign country. He has no friends here. Why should he stop to help?

But the stranger does stop.
He speaks kindly to the man in
foreign words, and helps him to
drink some water.

He washes his wounds and
carefully puts a bandage round
his head.

The stranger helps the man
up onto his donkey. He puts his
arm around him to stop him from
falling off, and gently leads him
down the path.

At the next town the stranger
finds an inn. He puts the man
to bed and pays the innkeeper.

'Look after him,' he says,
'until I get back.'

Jesus says, 'Which one was like a good neighbour?
The bishop, the judge or the stranger?'

Jesus said, 'There was once a rich man who had land which bore good crops. He began to think to himself, "I haven't anywhere to keep all my crops. What can I do? This is what I will do," he told himself; "I will tear down my barns and build bigger ones, where I will store my corn and all my other goods. Then I will say to myself, lucky man! You have all the good things you need for many years. Take life easy, eat, drink and enjoy yourself!" But God said to him, "You fool! This very night you will have to give up your life; then who will get all these things you have kept for yourself?"'

And Jesus concluded, 'This is how it is with those who pile up riches for themselves but are not rich in God's sight.'

Luke 12:16–21

The
Rich Farmer

Here is a farmer who is
very rich. The farmer is rich
because his soil is rich.
And his corn grows faster
than anyone else's.

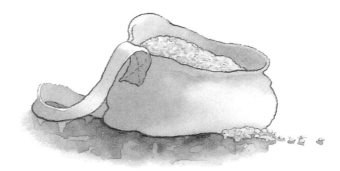

And higher than anyone else's.

And at harvest time he has much more of it than anyone else! Lucky man.

This year he has so much corn that his old barn can't hold it all. It is bursting at the seams.

'No problem,' says the farmer.
'I will pull it down and build
a bigger one. Then next year I
will be rich enough to take
life easy.'

So he builds a bigger barn.

But when harvest comes round again, the new barn is not big enough.

The greedy farmer has planted more corn than before. And carrots too.

'No problem,' says the farmer. 'I will build an even bigger, better barn. Then next year I will be richer still and then I can really enjoy myself.'

So he builds a bigger, better barn.

But at harvest time, even the bigger, better barn is not big enough.

Again the farmer has planted too much corn, too many carrots. (And a few cabbages as well.)

This time, the farmer says to himself, 'I will build the biggest, grandest barn the world has ever seen. And then I shall be so rich, I need never work again!'

The barn he builds reaches up to the sky. When it is finished the farmer sighs a great big sigh.

'Tomorrow I will gather in the harvest and then at last I shall begin to enjoy myself. I know! I'll have a party!'

But that very night he dies
in his sleep. Just like that!

The birds eat his corn,
the rabbits dig up his carrots
and his cabbages go to seed.

The big barn stands empty
and the rich farmer never does
get to enjoy his money.

Poor man.

Jesus says, 'How silly it is for a man to spend his whole life storing up riches for himself. To God, he is really a poor man.'